A WORD IN YOUR BEER

by
Colin Shaw

For Sue, with love
from Colin, Christmas, 2015
X X X

Chandler Press

First Published March 2011 by Chandler Press
Poppyseed Cottage, High Street, Stoke Ferry, Norfolk
PE33 9SF
chandlerpress@me.com

Printed by Cambridge Printers Ltd, Mercers Row,
Cambridge CB5 8HY

ISBN 978-0-9568282-0-0

For Robert Marx,
a better poet than I am

Thanks to Steph, Jackie and William
for help and warm words.

The cover illustration is by Alan Chadwick, for
whose artistry and time I am most grateful.

Acknowledgements
Dance the Viennese Waltz was published in *See Me,
Hear Me,* the People's Poet, 2002, and *Cloudburst,*
Cambridge Pub Poetry Group, 2005. The Tunnel of
Time appeared in *Not to be Forgotten,* Anchor
Books, 2005. Dog Days was published in *Poetry
From Eastern England,* Forward Press, 2006.
Jerusalem and Three Voices of Israel appeared in
New Life.

Contents

England

Is this still
a green and
pleasant land?
Set in a silver sea?
Where maidens and
their swains spin
and weave
their lustrous love
in silken bands?
In Arcadian bliss,
innocent as a kiss?

Poetic past can't
vouchsafe the future:
global warming
grips the land, spectral
desiccation stalks,
cities choke,
coasts dip and
crumble, gobbling
villages all-hallowed
by age.

What hope there is
rests with a
Down's syndrome
girl dancing
with an invisible
partner to jazz in a park
and men who weep
in front of television
in the dark.

Harmony

You see them round about, don't you?
Strong people, not a question of
muscularity, but of harmony:
Bald man in his Seventies apparently,
jumping over the doorstep boldly
grinning "I have to do this, don't I?"
Bent old woman with good leather bag
striding forward not looking round.
Stout-shoed man with beard
power-walking up the rise.
Greying gent leaning ahead slightly
as men do going to the pub warily,
edging along with silver duck-headed cane.
Cycling chipmunks
of all ages and genders.
Archaeologists to a man,
checking each other out fearlessly,
clustered loosely.
Maybe we're all strong,
headed the same way.
Maybe.

The Secret World

Sirens scream in
Cambridge rain:
What's going on?
Miscreants, mayhem, murder
on the roads?
All I do know is that away
from streets paced
by men with wild eyes
and fearful faces
lives a secret world.
Here, moorhens slip
into a clear stream
draining into the gentle Cam,
fearless at my tread.
A young girl passes
with flowered bag
full of innocent promise,
her face shrouded.
Songbirds startle
from hidden gardens.
No sirens here, thank God,
but only autumn grasses
sending their breath
heavenwards.

Crossing the Cam

Nirvana is intended,
as the priestly soul
of David
soars in incense calm
freely over the Cam.
No payment for
the Boatman,
or for the
unrecruited shadows
on the coffin-thin
narrowboat hailing me
on the other bank
as I watch
its reverent lights
pass on into
further dark.
Blessings were always
his answer and blessings
I say now.

Little gods

We have to be
little gods
if we are
to go to
the right place.

Lithe legs.
Chuck chuck
chuck chuck
chuck chuck

Chuck, chuck.

Widowed in Wells

He sits all
bulbousness and ears
at the bar,
speaking of friends
who will not come.
He talks to strangers
across the room
of things far and wide,
of rare birds spied,
of a three-master
called the Albatross
ghosting into the old
smugglers' port
in the dark.
They say it carries drugs
from Holland.

A barnacled crab
washed up on the shore,
he marvels at the geese
flying their rites
of passage
in formulaic 'Vs',
him a straggler left behind.

Silverton

Gravestones tongue
their certainties
and in the parish magazine
it is written
Miss Mogg
was kind to plants
and also
supported the Seamen's Mission.
Her reedy,
blue-veined arms
among the lobelias
soothed their cares,
won their love.

The church clock
measures out
the dreaming morning
with parsimony.
Birds dive
like dying thoughts.

Towards
the browsing hills
where bees
suck hollyhock hearts
speeds a train,
its sudden shadow
consuming the wheatfields
like black flame.

Jerusalem

In old Jerusalem the peace of bells
tells lies.
Here in the main flesh of Israel
the heart sighs
for the real peace it has never known,
nor will know.
But it pretends. Devoted feet whisper
to the shrines
of their several true gods.
Countless times
these holy cradles have been snatched:
they expect it.
Perhaps it has its own kind of rest,
of patience.
A city with time on its side is
unimpressed
by a procession of conquerors and heroes.
The gates shut
and the tide of passion rolls past.
Inside, unaffected,
the voices of the Dome and the Holy
Sepulchre
rustle in unison:
they have their own communion.

The wind bears
other voices, of old friends,
Armenian, Greek, Hebrew, Arabic,
quiet, trusting.
The tired stones have forgiven each other
over centuries.

Three voices of Israel

By the green waters
of Galilea
where Jesus walked
for love
the young Sarah printed
in the sand
the only words
she knew:
'I cannot kiss
my brother Ismail
because I may not
love him.'

In the empty church
at Nazareth
where Jesus talked
of hope
the young Ismail
spoke the only
words he knew:
'I have no hope.'

In the quiet streets
of Jerusalem
where Jesus died
for peace
the young warrior
spoke the only
words he knew:
'I wanted to watch
the wounded Arab die,
but now I know
Jew and Arab
have the same blood
and cry the same cry.'

Harvest

I sat at night
high in mountains;
my harvest of tears
drenched
the moonwhite rocks.
The salt grains
wore steps down
to the sighing sea.
It was my only crop.

The Tunnel of Time

So. How is it looking down
the tunnel of time?
Mmm.
A writery sort of fellow
with a certain callow
charm. Reasonable luck
with the ladies.
What was the score?
Thirty-five, three inside
marriage, outside sin.
I know a bloke who counted up
a thousand, but then he was Irish.

What else?
Mmm.
Difficult to say.
My brother's bud mouth pursed
for a pint before he embraced death.

Sometimes empty spaces
predominate in which strange
things whorled. These whirligigs
have a name, but I've forgotten.

With this sort of head it's difficult
to remember names looking down
the tunnel of time.
Does it matter?
There's a hazy figure looming
over my pram in blitzed London.
I'm told he was my grandfather,
officered on the battlefield
of the War to end all Wars.
Gran remembered Gladstone and Disraeli
as she looked down her tunnel,
my tunnel too.

When the noise ceases

What happens when the noise ceases?
When the Babel shuts the fuck up?
When the mobile is switched onto voicemail
for whatever ever is?
When the talk, talk, talk
I hear coming from my lollilips
dries up?
When the world's banalities
empty into blank screens?

Will I be swept up into the arms
of Saint Peter and all the saints
as I emerge from the warm
conduit of love?
Will there be a clamour of angels,
hosts of grinning departed relatives,
old loves, hands held out?

I hope not, I hope not.
What I want when the noise ceases
is to hide in the Seven Sleepers den.

Pub Moment

Off-beam talk,
thoughts a-whirring,
the dead interfering.
As though drunk –
but not enough pawk
was around,
with little drink
going down.
Just unsettled, disconnected,
weather concurring.
We were surely
half-way here,
half-way to heaven.

Pawk: *Scots/N. England dialect for sauciness,
especially humorous, the kind of craic usual among
friends in pubs. Origin unknown.*

Dog Days

In the eternal universe of the
infernal internet, in my dog days,
I hoard old G2s,
Observers, scraps of a life
half-remembered,
half-sought.
Parings of thoughts drag me down
further,
in my dog days.
Not to despair,
but somewhere beyond
and beneath.
It doesn't matter
where precisely.
In my dog days,
I mourn lost loves,
girls with green eyes
and Paris girls
with eyes that killed.
I mourn them and
their utter lostness
in my dog days.
But a bead slides
down the page
in blessing of
my dogdayness.

Dance the Viennese Waltz

Dance the Viennese waltz
whirl to the music box
bodies grafted
swirling through the rising mist
heads falling back
in easy laughter.

Dance
dance
after wine
in the late summer
eyes locked
in a trance
and as you turn
figures on a wedding cake
the camera fixes
your china smiles.

Dance
your golden dance
spin like
fallen leaves
on a river.

Dance the dance
you must
her dress lifting
to brush
the watching shadows.

Peacocks
dream high in scented trees
under a crescent moon
and squirrels
fly with flashing eyes
and tails bright
with sparks
to guide
your manic feet.

Dance dance
till you drop.

In praise of pubs

What a blessing is a well-run pub.
There the almond-eyed young
can taste the magic potions
of Bud Ice, Red Stripe tops,
Vodka Hooch, Tiger,
Norfolk Norkie and triple Jamiesons.
Egyptoid, speaking in hieroglyphics,
they take on the strength
of ancient gods.

Wibbly-wobbly girl

A girl with a
wibbly-wobbly
bottom and a
wibbly-wobbly
ribbon on her
ankle goes
wibbly-wobbling by,
all wibbly-wobbling
in my eye.

The Bookworm

You know how you look
at all those shelves
crammed with books
and worry about how
many you'll read
before – well, you know?
Don't you fret about
all those others
you want to sniff as they
are freshly minted?
Worry because once there was
all the time in the world
and you didn't seize it?

But if you can hold the future
in still mind's gaze
maybe the worries
can be borne,
the moment fixed,
mortality stayed
in Shepherd's care.

The Last Voyage of The Kantara

Déjeuner sur La Kantara
en route de St. Malo à Tanger
le 8 Avril, 1913.
Première Classe:

Apéritifs, olives variées
–

Langue de Boeuf
Sauce Piquante
–

Omelette Paysanne
–

Trou Normand
–

Epaule d'Agneau
Bourée de Cèpes
–

Légumes Printanières rôties
–

Sorbet
–

Fromages Régionales
–

Café et Petits Fours
–

Vin à Volunté.

****

Forecast for Bay of Biscay South, six
o'clock, April 8th, 1913:
Storm Force 10 approaching from North.
Winds gusting up to
50 knots, worsening. Visibility poor,
deteriorating.
North Cones and Drums hoisted
by French Coast Guard.

Holy Feet

Feet go up
on pilgrimage
to the torn curtain
bearing bodies hungry
for wafer and wine
in a tempoed dance:
Feet fervent,
feet in unison,
feet on air,
feet stumbling and
shuffling in age,
feet certain in
shiny shoes knowing
why they're there,
feet tippy-toe or
tapping to rhythms inside.

The swing

The swing bears
an invisible body
as it's pulled like a
tolled bell
next to the church.
Who's on it?
Is it God having fun?
He's got to sometimes.

Cro-Magnon Cambridge Man

'I don't know ya!
So I won't talk to ya.
Though you smile and say "mornin'"
I don't know ya.
Two-way chat is off the agenda
when I don't know ya.
I may give pleasantries an uppity smile
but response is out
when I don't know ya.
I'm a Cambridge man, so
why should I want to know ya?'

Spider

A spider knows
more than I,
ambitiously building
bright steely webs
across unlikely
spaces endlessly.

Shatter its dreams
of conquest and it picks
itself up again, measures
the span and begins to
draw once more on air
as if to spite us.

We can crush
a spider. Yet, when the
mushroom cloud ascends,
it will be the survivor.

Maybe the web comes
before the host.
An old African proverb
goes: With love and care
the spider web weaves
its spider.
What can we say of our
love and care?

Mating, like ours,
is an elaborate joke by God.
Courtship is choreographed
on her silken bed,
delicate touches of 16
translucent legs
and four palps.
Warily, the male advances
to test her mood,
saucy or hungry
for his flesh.
Satisfied her lust is
just for sex, he jets
his sperm into his ready palps.
She cocks four legs
mantis-like round her head
offering her epigyne
for his inspection and delight.
Climax comes as a shiver
of intertwined limbs.
Unlike us, the union
brings no chlamydia.

Little Bird

A little bird perched
on my shoulder:
Snub nose,
button mouth,
cocky eyes,
fat thighs,
black stockings,
short skirt,
flapping tie,
white shirt.
Then she blew.

Space Refusenik

I won't go
to C185X winking
at its sister
200,000 light years away
among the septillions
of stars I fix wonderingly
with my gaze as overloaded
Earth gutters out.

I don't want
to download my
consciousness onto
a virtual body
in cyberspace
for the journey-too-far.
And the soul's just a theory.
Nor do I want to be
stuffed dreamless
in a deep freeze
like fish fingers.

Long ago stargazers
saw our survival in
voyaging to the edge.
But that would mean imperialism,
and what if the natives
weren't friendly and JC
hadn't visited yet?

Terraforming needs devotion
and the kiss of Love.

The end times will come
to Mother Earth
one way or another,
through meteor target practice
or becoming crispy duck
when swollen Apollo
takes us in his embrace.

No. I'll await fulfilment of those
unbelievable promises made in start times:
They're just as good a guess as any.
Who knows what or who'll get me.

Anyway, however we dice it,
our particular universe will collapse
like a climaxing spunk-bag.